THE PHANTOM HITCHHIKER

and other Ghost Mysteries

THE PHANTOM HITCHHIKER

and other Ghost Mysteries

DANIEL COHEN
ILLUSTRATED BY ELSIE LENNOX

SCHOLASTIC INC.
New York Toronto London Auckland Sydney

ISBN 0-590-93712-X

Text copyright © 1995 by Daniel Cohen.
Illustrations copyright © 1995 by Elsie Lennox.
All rights reserved. Published by Scholastic Inc., 555 Broadway, New York, NY 10012, by arrangement with Larousse Kingfisher Chambers Inc.

12 11 10 9 8 7 6 5 4   3 4 5 6 7 8 9/0

Printed in the U.S.A.   40

First Scholastic printing, September 1996

◆ Contents ◆

The Ghost of Raynham Hall   7

The Flying Dutchman   11

Abraham Lincoln   15

The Radiant Boy   19

The Haunted U-Boat   23

Screaming Skulls   30

The Voodoo Queen of New Orleans   34

Spectral Hounds   37

The Curse of the Octagon   41

The Tower of London   46

Admiral Tryon Returns   50

A Vision of Death   56

The Phantom Hitchhiker   60

DO YOU BELIEVE IN GHOSTS?

Here are thirteen (a nice round number) accounts of strange and ghostly events. They range from haunted castles and demon dogs to skulls that don't like to be moved. These are the sort of events that make you think, make you wonder, and make you hesitate just a bit longer before entering a darkened room.

◆ The Ghost of ◆ Raynham Hall

Picture the scene: a magnificent mansion at the dead of night in Norfolk, England. The year is 1786. The Prince Regent, later to become King George IV, is staying as guest of honor. Suddenly, a bloodcurdling scream rings out. It is the prince, dressed only in his nightshirt, running out of his room and down the stairway.

This may sound like the opening scene of a horror movie: in fact, this was a real event that left the future king in a terrified state. He woke everybody in the house and announced that he would not spend another hour there. He got dressed, and followed by his many servants he left. And true to his word he never came back. As you may have guessed by now, the house was

haunted. That night the prince was sure he had
seen, standing by his bed, the famous Brown
Lady of Raynham Hall, a ghost whose identity
remains a mystery to this day.

During the Christmas season of 1835 a
Colonel Loftus said he had got a good look at
the ghost. He described her as being a noble-
looking lady wearing a brown satin dress. Her

face was bathed in an unearthly light. But what was truly frightening about her was that she had no eyes—only empty sockets where the eyes should have been.

Colonel Loftus made a sketch of what he had seen and a painting was made from the sketch. The picture was hung in the room where the ghost was most frequently seen.

A few years after Colonel Loftus's experience, the novelist Frederick Marryat was staying at Raynham Hall. He had heard stories about the ghost and was eager to try and catch a glimpse of her. He asked if he could sleep in the "haunted room" where the painting hung. One evening Marryat and two companions saw a strange figure carrying a lamp gliding along an upstairs corridor. They hid behind a door. Light from the lamp reflected off the figure's brown dress, and as she passed the door she turned her eyeless face toward them and grinned in a "diabolical manner."

Marryat happened to be carrying a pistol. He fired point blank at the terrifying figure. If someone had been trying to play a joke, Marryat was sure they would have been shot dead. But the bullet passed right through the figure, which promptly disappeared.

The most famous appearance of the ghost came in 1936 when two photographers from the magazine *Country Life* were taking pictures of the interior of Raynham Hall. They were photographing the main stairway of the house when the shadowy figure of what appeared to be a woman in a veil came down the stairs. They took a picture, and when it was developed it showed a dim and ghostly looking figure on the stairs. The film was examined by experts at the time, who stated it was not a fake.

This picture of the Brown Lady of Raynham Hall is considered to be one of the best and most puzzling of the many photographs that people claim to have taken of ghosts.

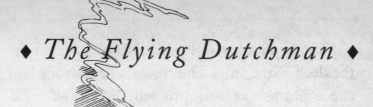

◆ *The Flying Dutchman* ◆

Perhaps the legend began with a 16th-century Dutch sea captain named Cornelius Vanderdecken. Or it may have been a somewhat later Dutch captain called Bernard Fokke. Wherever and whenever it began, the legend of the *Flying Dutchman* has become the most famous of all tales of phantom ships.

As sailors tell the tale, while sailing around the Cape of Good Hope, the southern tip of Africa, the Dutch captain's ship encountered a terrible storm. The frightened crew pleaded with the captain to find a safe harbor. The captain not only refused, he mocked their fear. He bragged that he was afraid of nothing on earth or in heaven.

Then suddenly a glowing figure appeared on the deck of the ship. The crew was awestruck but the captain was unimpressed. "Who wants a peaceful passage?" he shouted. "I don't!" Then he threatened to shoot the figure.

When the figure did not move, the captain drew his pistol and fired, but the gun exploded in his hand. The mysterious figure then put a curse on the captain, saying that he was doomed to sail forever, without rest. "And since it is your delight to torment sailors," declared the figure, "you shall torment them, for you shall be the evil spirit of the sea. Your ship shall bring misfortune to all who sight it."

And, so the legend goes, any ship unlucky enough to spot the Dutch captain's phantom ship will either be lost at sea or experience some other calamity.

The story of the *Flying Dutchman* has been retold in many forms from poems to films. It has even been made into an opera. But there have also been many sightings of the phantom ship reported by experienced sailors.

Of all the sightings, the best known was made in 1881 by the man who was to become King George V of England. He was serving

aboard the *Baccante* when in July:

"The *Flying Dutchman* crossed our bows. A strange red light appeared, as of a phantom ship all aglow, in the midst of which light the masts, spars, and sails of a brig two hundred yards distant stood up in strong relief. . . . On arriving there, no vestige nor any sign whatever of any material ship was to be seen either near or right away to the horizon, the night being clear and the sea calm. Thirteen persons altogether saw her."

Shortly after the encounter the first man to have sighted the ship fell to his death from the mast. The admiral aboard the *Baccante* became ill and died before the end of the voyage.

◆ *Abraham Lincoln* ◆

There are more ghostly tales told about America's first murdered president than about any other figure in American history. The fatal shooting of Lincoln while he was at the theater in 1865, and other events in his life, attracted such stories.

Soon after the end of World War II, Queen Wilhelmina of the Netherlands was staying at the White House. One night she heard a knock at her door. The hour was late, so she assumed that it must be something important. She opened the door and saw Abraham Lincoln standing there. The queen fainted with shock.

A number of people have claimed to have felt Lincoln's ghostly presence around the White

House. President Theodore Roosevelt reported seeing Lincoln's spirit in several different rooms. Grace Coolidge, wife of President Calvin Coolidge, described seeing a figure, "in black, with a stole draped across his shoulders to ward off the drafts and chills of Washington's night air."

Eleanor Roosevelt, wife of President Franklin D. Roosevelt, denied that she had ever actually seen Lincoln, but she did have a story about one of her staff members. Her secretary was passing what had been Lincoln's bedroom and saw a familiar-looking lanky figure sitting on the bed pulling on his boots. When the secretary checked, it was discovered that no guest was staying in that room. On another occasion Roosevelt's valet apparently ran from the White House shouting that he had just seen Lincoln's ghost.

The Lincoln bedroom was the room that was traditionally given to visiting heads of state. Winston Churchill never liked sleeping there when he visited the White House, and in the morning he would regularly be found sleeping in a room across the hall. He never said why.

Lincoln was a melancholy man whose life had often been touched by tragedy. His favorite son, twelve-year-old Willie, died halfway through Lincoln's first term of office. The death deeply affected Lincoln and nearly shattered his wife Mary. Willie's weeping ghost has been reported around the White House on several occasions.

The night before his assassination it is said that Lincoln dreamed of his own death. After his murder, many spirit mediums (people who claim to have the power to communicate with the dead) said that they were in contact with Lincoln.

There was a great craze in the late 1800s for what was known as spirit photography. People mistakenly thought that a camera could not be tricked, and that a photograph proved a ghost's existence. Many cheating photographers created fake pictures with ghostly figures (in fact, they were usually dummies or assistants in costume) hovering in the background. Abraham Lincoln was one of the most popular subjects of spirit photographs, adding to the general belief that he had returned to this world in phantom form!

After Lincoln's death, his body was taken back to Springfield, Illinois, aboard a special funeral train. All along the route people lined up to see the train pass; it became a sort of national funeral procession. Ever since then, according to legend, a ghostly train takes the same route every year. The train is covered with black streamers, and the engine is crewed by skeletons.

◆ *The Radiant Boy* ◆

Here is a strange story from the late 18th century. A young army officer, Captain Robert Stewart, second son of the Marquis of Londonderry, was out hunting when he became lost during a storm.

He asked for shelter in a large house nearby. The house was already filled with guests, but the owner told Captain Stewart that he was sure the butler would find room for him somewhere. After dinner Captain Stewart was shown to a bedroom which looked as if it had not been used for a long time. But it was quite comfortable and there was a good fire in the fireplace. Stewart was very tired and fell asleep almost immediately.

Later that night he was woken by an

amazingly bright light. At first he thought the room must be on fire. Then he saw the glowing form of a boy who was standing near the bed gazing at him. As he watched, the light and the boy's form began to fade until finally they disappeared.

Stewart was a suspicious man and thought someone was playing a trick on him. In the morning he angrily told his host what had happened. His host looked shocked, and was even more startled when the butler admitted that he had put Stewart in "the boy's room" because there was no place else for him to sleep.

Stewart was then told

this story. The glowing form was the ghost of a boy of about nine or ten who had once lived in the house and had been murdered by his mother during a fit of madness. The appearance of the flaming phantom was an evil omen to anyone who saw it. It meant the person would have a period of great power and prosperity. But at the height of their power they would die violently.

This news didn't worry Stewart. As a second son he did not expect much prosperity or power. As a soldier the possibility of a violent death was something he had always accepted.

But within a few years his life changed dramatically. His older brother drowned in a boating accident and Stewart became the family heir, adopting the title of Viscount Castlereagh. He then left the army and went into politics. He displayed an extraordinary talent for government and rose rapidly to become one of the most powerful men in England.

Castlereagh, as he came to be known, had always been a cold and untrusting man. The enormous pressures and responsibilities that were heaped upon him only made him worse. He began to feel that everyone was plotting against him. Finally his behavior became so bizarre that he was confined to his country home. Despite being guarded, Viscount Castlereagh eventually killed himself in a fit of madness.

The prophecy made so many years earlier had been fulfilled.

There are many other stories of these glowing ghostly figures, called Radiant Boys, from England and throughout northern Europe. The figures are always considered omens of sudden and violent death.

◆ *The Haunted U-Boat* ◆

During World War I the submarine, then commonly called the underwater boat or U-boat, had become an enormously successful weapon for the Germans. In 1916 the Germans were rushing to complete twenty-four new U-boats. Construction on twenty-three of them was uneventful. But for the twenty-fourth, known only by its number, U-65, there was nothing but trouble.

Several workmen were killed in accidents during construction. In October of 1916 when U-65 was launched, one of its officers fell or was swept overboard and drowned. During its first underwater test something—no one was ever able to discover what—went wrong and the ship was unable to surface for twelve hours. Water seeped into the ship and entered the engine, creating poisonous fumes. The captain and crew barely survived. The very next day a torpedo exploded on deck and a second lieutenant and five other crewmen were killed.

Because of all the accidents, U-65 picked up the reputation of being a bad-luck or jinx ship. And there were tales that the dead second lieutenant had been seen. One man said, "We saw him come aboard and walk slowly to the bow. He stood there, staring at us, with his arms folded across his chest."

The U-boat commander realized how quickly rumors like this could upset the crew. He told his men, "I'm sure it's just imagination. The accident was a sad experience for all of us. Just try and put it out of your minds." One man couldn't. After reporting that he had seen the ghost, he deserted the ship and was never found.

Nothing out of the ordinary happened to U-65 for the next few months. Then the crew began reporting the ghost again. The ship docked at the port of Bruges in Belgium for routine maintenance, and captain and crew went ashore. There was an attack on the city and the

U-boat captain was killed.

This strengthened U-65's reputation as a jinx ship. But the German navy was in dire need of every U-boat. The ship was checked again on the theory that fumes might be causing hallucinations among the crew. Nothing was found. Admiral Schroeder, who was head of the U-boat command, took the unusual step of spending a night aboard U-65. He assured the crew that he had slept very well and had not been disturbed by ghosts. Even so, a chaplain was called aboard to drive away, or exorcise, the ghost. Then, Lieutenant Commander Gustav Schelle, a believer in strict crew discipline, was chosen as the new commander. He said that anyone who reported seeing a ghost would be severely punished.

For a year there were no more reports of ghosts. Then the sightings began once again. One of the most trusted officers on the ship, Master Gunner Erich Eberhardt, rushed into the control room screaming, "I've seen the ghost— an officer standing near the bow torpedo tubes. He brushed past me and disappeared." The master gunner was in such a terrified state that he had to be locked up. A few hours later, still hysterical with fear, he killed himself.

The next tragedy to hit the submarine was the death of Chief Petty Officer Richard Meyer, who was swept overboard. His body was never recovered.

Morale on the U-boat was now at its lowest point. U-65 tried to avoid all contact with the enemy. But the ship was still struck by shellfire

and had to limp back to Bruges for repairs. Admiral Schroeder was furious. He had Captain Schelle and every other officer of U-65 removed, and when she went to sea again in mid-1918, U-65 had a completely different staff of officers and a new crew.

The end of U-65 came mysteriously. On the morning of July 10, 1918, an American submarine patrolling off the southern coast of Ireland saw a German U-boat lying on its side on the surface. The ship was identified as U-65.

The Americans thought the ship might be a decoy that had been booby-trapped, so they watched it carefully for a long time. The ship seemed to be deserted and the American captain decided that the safest thing to do was blow it up. As they were preparing the torpedo, U-65 was torn apart by a violent explosion.

Was U-65 really a decoy filled with explosives that went off too soon, or was there some other reason for the explosion? Just before she blew up, the American submarine captain said he thought he saw a figure standing on the ship near the bow. It appeared to be a German officer wearing a navy overcoat. He stood unmoving with his arms folded across his chest.

The war ended a few months later and all the other German U-boats surrendered peacefully. Over the years the case of U-65 has been investigated repeatedly. No one has ever been able to find satisfactory explanations for the strange and ghostly events.

◆ *Screaming Skulls* ◆

There are many stories from around the world about the chilling, even dangerous things that can happen when the remains of the dead are disturbed. Some of the spookiest stories are about "screaming skulls" which, according to tradition, protest loudly if they are moved from their usual place.

In Britain, the most famous of these skulls is found at Wardley Hall in Manchester. The skull is supposed to be that of Robert Downes, who in the 17th century had his head cut off during a drunken brawl on London Bridge. The head was then sent to his widow in Manchester. At Wardley Hall the skull is kept in a locked cupboard behind the main stairs of the hall.

According to one visitor, "There is a tradition that if the skull is removed or ill-used, some uncommon noise or disturbance always follows, to the terror of the whole house."

Another "screaming skull" is a permanent resident of a farmhouse in southern England. It is supposed to scream whenever anyone tries to bury it. According to the most widely believed tradition, the skull is that of a servant who said his spirit would never rest until his body was taken back to his native Africa. This was not done. Instead the body was buried in the local graveyard.

After the burial, terrible screams issued from the grave, and the house in which the servant had lived rattled and creaked. Finally the restless corpse was dug up and placed in the house. That ended the noises, but the people who lived in the house did not like sharing it with an unburied corpse. So there were three more attempts to re-bury the body, all with the same eerie results.

Finally, the owners of the house gave up and kept the body, now reduced to a skeleton, in the house. Over the years bits and pieces of the skeleton gradually disappeared, until only the skull remained.

In a farmhouse in Derbyshire, England, there is a skull that is apparently very sensitive to its surroundings. A mid-19th-century account states:

"Twice within the memory of man, the skull has been taken from the premises; once on building the present house on the site of the old one, and another time, when an attempt was made to bury it in the chapel graveyard. But there was no peace, no rest! It had to be replaced."

The skull of murderer William Corder, who was hanged in 1826, was stolen by a scientist named Dr. Kilner who studied the human body.

He kept the skull in a polished wooden box in his study. A little while later strange things began happening in the doctor's house. There were mysterious noises and finally the wooden box exploded, but the skull was undamaged.

Dr. Kilner tried to get rid of the grisly relic. He gave it to a retired prison official named Hopkins who already owned, among other souvenirs of the crime, the gallows upon which Corder was hanged. "Perhaps it won't harm you to look after his skull," Dr. Kilner wrote.

He was wrong. Hopkins and the doctor had nothing but bad luck, and within a few months both were bankrupt. Finally Hopkins arranged to have the skull buried in a graveyard. After that, the run of bad luck for the two men ended.

The Voodoo Queen
◆ of New Orleans ◆

Even today a visitor to New Orleans's historic French Quarter can find obscure little shops selling voodoo charms, powders, and oils. But during the 19th century the presence of voodoo could be felt everywhere in the old sections of the city.

Those skilled in the practice of voodoo were consulted by the rich and the poor, and by slaves and their masters. The voodoo priests and priestesses were greatly respected and greatly feared. And no one had a more powerful and fearful reputation than a woman called Marie Laveau, the voodoo queen of New Orleans.

Like everything else about the secretive practice of voodoo, the history of Marie Laveau is shadowy and obscure. No one knows who she really was, where she came from, how old she was when she died—or if she really died at all. But there is no doubt there was at least one person who called herself Marie Laveau.

She was first heard of presiding over voodoo dances at a place in New Orleans called Congo Square, in the 1830s. From her little house on St. Anne Street she sold powerful magical charms and potions. Members of some of New Orleans's leading families were said to have visited St. Anne Street under cover of darkness to buy potions that would help them find a lover, or get rid of one.

Fifty years later Marie was still holding voodoo ceremonies and selling charms at the St. Anne Street house, and witnesses said that she didn't look a day older than she had in the 1830s. Marie disappeared in the 1890s after New Orleans was struck by a hurricane. According to some legends, Marie, protected by her magic, couldn't be killed. She simply went away for her own mysterious reasons. Some people believed she may have changed herself into a crow or some other animal.

Historians think that the answer to Marie's

"eternal" youth may be that there were *two* Marie Laveaus. The original Marie died in 1881, after which another woman, perhaps her daughter, continued practicing voodoo and selling charms for another ten years or so, under the same name.

At the old St. Louis cemetery in New Orleans there are two unmarked tombs, and many people think that the original Marie Laveau is buried in one of them, though no one is sure which one. Even today people often leave voodoo offerings on the tombs.

There are regular reports that Marie's ghost has been seen in the vicinity of the cemetery. One person said that the indignant ghost hit him

across the face when he failed to recognize her.

The site of Marie's old house at 1020 St. Anne Street is also supposed to be haunted by the ghosts of the voodoo queen and her followers, who can still be heard performing their rituals from beyond the grave.

◆ *Spectral Hounds* ◆

"Footprints."

"A man's or a woman's?"

Dr. Mortimer looked strangely at us for an instant, and his voice sank almost to a whisper as he answered:

"Mr. Holmes, they were the footprints of a gigantic hound!"

This passage is from the most famous of all the Sherlock Holmes novels, *The Hound of the Baskervilles*. The story itself is fiction; the tradition behind it may not be.

Arthur Conan Doyle, creator of Sherlock Holmes, first got his idea for this tale in 1901 from his friend Fletcher Robinson. Robinson told him the story of a spectral or phantom

hound that was supposed to roam the bleak moors of Dartmoor in England. And that is where Conan Doyle set his story.

Similar tales are told all over the British Isles; indeed they are told all over the world. They are so common that some people wonder if they are more than just legends.

These phantom dogs are known by many names. In southern England the dog is called Black Shuck and is said to have a single gleaming eye in the center of its forehead. In the north of England it is known as Skriker, the Trash-hound, or Padfoot. In many places it is just called the Black Dog.

In the English town of Tring, tradition has it that a phantom dog appears there from time to time at the place where a woman was once hanged for witchcraft many hundreds of years ago. Here is an early 19th-century description of the animal:

"I then saw an immense black dog just in front of our house. It was the strangest-looking creature I ever saw. He was as big as a Newfoundland dog, but very thin and shaggy.

He had long ears, a long tail, and eyes like balls of fire. When he opened his mouth we could see long teeth. He seemed to grin at us. In a few minutes the dog disappeared, seeming to vanish like a shadow, or to sink into the earth."

Not all of the stories of these phantom dogs are hundreds of years old. In 1978 a woman told this story:

"Then we saw, coming up the hill toward us on the right-hand side of the road, the most extraordinary dog. It was a German shepherd type but with long dirty white hair which stood up around it in spikes, as if frozen. It looked almost transparent. Its eyes were red and glowing. Not many dogs make you exclaim as you pass them and still, when I think of it I get goose bumps."

Within a few months the woman's husband died unexpectedly. Later the woman met someone else who said they had seen this dog and that a tragedy had followed.

Even today, there are people who believe that a phantom dog is an omen of death. Others are not convinced. . . .

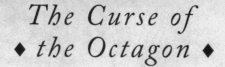

The Curse of
♦ the Octagon ♦

At about the time the White House was built in Washington, D.C. in the 1790s, John Tayloe, a wealthy Virginia planter, had a mansion built in the city. The house was called the Octagon—though no one seems to know why. Octagon means "eight-sided" but the house has only six sides. It is one of the most historic houses in Washington, and there are many stories of hauntings within its walls.

Shortly after the house was built, one of the Tayloe girls fell in love with a British army officer. At the time, relations between the United States and Britain were still very tense because of the American Revolution fought between them ten years before. John Tayloe would not even

allow the officer to enter his house. Father and daughter quarreled bitterly.

One evening, after an argument with her father, the girl took her candle and rushed up the staircase from the main hall. When she had nearly reached the top, there was a scream and she plunged down the stairwell and landed in the hall. The girl was dead, and to this day, no one knows how she fell.

On some stormy nights a candle was seen flickering on the stairs. Then there was a girl's scream followed by the sound of something hitting the floor.

A few years after the death of the first Tayloe girl, the second suffered an eerily similar fate. She too had been quarreling with her father. They would not speak, and barely looked at one another. One evening they met on the stairs. The daughter tried to get out of her father's way, but lost her balance. She tumbled down the stairs to her death. People automatically avoided the place at the foot of the stairs where her body came to rest. It gave them an uncomfortable feeling.

Some years later, during the War of 1812 between Britain and the United States, Washington was invaded and the White House burned. The Octagon became the temporary home of President James Madison. His lively wife Dolly was a celebrated hostess, and when the war ended, some of her best parties were held in the Octagon to celebrate. For years afterward people said they could hear the rumble of ghostly coaches coming up the gravel driveway, and the

murmuring voices of unseen guests. Some people reported seeing the semitransparent figure of Dolly Madison herself, wearing the feathered turban which she made famous.

One part of the house was continually disturbed by a thumping sound. Later, when repairs were being made, the skeleton of a young woman was found behind one of the walls. It was

said to be the remains of a servant girl killed by her lover and hidden to conceal the crime. After the skeleton was given a proper burial the noises were not heard again.

Many other violent events were associated with the Octagon. At one point it was owned by a gambler who was shot by someone he cheated. His ghost has been seen reaching for a gun. The house may have been used as a hiding place for runaway slaves and as a hospital during the Civil War. Sounds of sobbing and moaning were said to come from the ghosts of the slaves and wounded soldiers.

The house acquired such a bad reputation that no one would live in it. By 1900 the place was empty and falling apart. It was taken over by a group devoted to preserving Washington's historic buildings, and the Octagon was restored to its former glory. Since the restorations, few ghosts have been seen, or unexplained sounds heard, though every once in a while someone reports seeing Dolly Madison in her turban.

◆ *The Tower of London* ◆

The Tower of London has been the scene of a great deal of history—much of it tragic and bloody. There have been so many executions, murders, and other dark deeds carried out within the walls of this massive and gloomy castle that it is no wonder there are many ghostly tales attached to it.

The most famous execution to take place at the Tower was the beheading of Anne Boleyn, King Henry VIII's second wife, in 1536. The ghost of Anne, both with and without her head, has often been reported at the Tower.

The best documented sighting came in 1864. While the captain of the guards was making his rounds, he found one of his men unconscious.

When the guard was awakened he told of seeing a woman in a white gown coming out of the chamber in which Anne had spent the last night before her execution. The figure had glided toward the guard, who called out for it to stop, but it continued to walk right at him. So he had stabbed at it with his bayonet, and the bayonet had gone right through it. Then he knew he was facing a ghost and had fainted.

The captain of the guard didn't think much of this story. He believed the man had fallen asleep while on duty and had made up the ghostly woman in white. The guard was to be court-martialed for neglecting his post.

During the proceedings, however, other guards testified that they had witnessed the entire scene, and that the figure had disappeared as soon as the man fainted. Some guards reported that they had seen the ghostly figure on other occasions when they had been on duty near that room. The "ghost defense" worked and the case against the guard was dismissed.

In 1483 two royal princes, twelve-year-old

Edward V and his ten-year-old brother Richard, were imprisoned in the Tower of London by their uncle Richard, the Duke of Gloucester. They were never heard from again, and with them out of the way Gloucester took the throne as King Richard III. Many historians believe Richard had the princes murdered—but there is no solid evidence that he did.

For almost two centuries the Tower was said to be haunted by the ghosts of the princes. Then in 1674 a wooden chest containing the skeletons of two boys was found in the Tower. These remains were given a royal burial, and the boys' ghosts have not troubled the Tower since.

The ghost of Sir Walter Raleigh, who was imprisoned in the Tower of London for thirteen years, is also said to walk along the walls near the room in which he was kept.

Guy Fawkes, who in 1605 tried unsuccessfully to blow up the Houses of Parliament, was horribly tortured and finally executed in the Tower. Some say his screams can still be heard echoing through the gloomy corridors at night.

Admiral Tryon
◆ Returns ◆

On June 22, 1893 Admiral Sir George Tryon made a colossal blunder which resulted in one of the greatest and most unnecessary tragedies in naval history.

Admiral Tryon was commander of a fleet of ships in the Mediterranean, and was conducting maneuvers off the coast of Tripoli. He issued orders to his fleet of eleven ships from aboard his flagship HMS *Victoria*. As part of the maneuvers he ordered his ships to form two parallel columns. The *Victoria* was at the head of one column while the battleship HMS *Camperdown*, under Rear Admiral Albert Markham, headed the other.

Admiral Tryon then ordered the two

columns of ships to reverse direction by turning inward toward one another. This was a standard naval maneuver, and it would have been perfectly safe if the two columns had been widely separated from one another. But they were so close that the ships were obviously going to collide. To make matters worse, the *Camperdown* had a steel ram in her bow, so that during a battle she could deliberately ram other ships and sink them.

All the officers aboard the *Victoria* could see what would happen if the admiral's order to turn inward were to be carried out. But no one dared step forward to contradict Tryon.

Admiral Markham also knew the order was

dangerous and he hesitated before carrying it out. But from the *Victoria* came the message, "What are you waiting for?"

And so Markham began the maneuver, hoping that Admiral Tryon had some other plan in mind and at the last moment would change his instructions.

As the two huge warships bore down on one another Admiral Tryon was looking in the other direction. When the ships were only two hundred yards apart Admiral Markham finally gave the order to stop and reverse direction. By that time Admiral Tryon also seems to have realized that something was horribly wrong and he gave the same order. But it was too late. At exactly 3:43 P.M. the *Camperdown*'s bow sliced into the *Victoria*, creating a tremendous gash. The water poured in and within minutes the

Victoria began to sink.

The well-trained crew of the *Victoria* remained perfectly calm and tried to board the lifeboats, but there wasn't enough time. Some 355 of the 600 officers and men aboard the *Victoria* died as a result of the collision. In the best tradition of the sea, Admiral Tryon went down with his ship. He remained at his post on the bridge and never told anyone what he had intended to do, but he was heard to say: "It's all my fault—entirely my fault."

In London that evening, unaware of the disaster, Lady Tryon gave a reception in the couple's elegant house in Eaton Square. At the height of the festivities, a large and heavy-set man wearing an admiral's full uniform came down the main staircase and began greeting the guests, many of whom he knew by name. Everyone who saw him certainly knew who he was—Admiral Sir George Tryon.

Lady Tryon never saw the figure. A number of people came up to her and told her how nice it was to see Sir George again. When she told them that her husband was not at the reception but aboard HMS *Victoria* in the Mediterranean they didn't believe her. They had just seen the admiral with their own eyes.

In fact, by the time the guests reported seeing Admiral Tryon, his body lay at the bottom of the Mediterranean.

News of the *Victoria* disaster did not reach London until the following morning. To this day, no one really knows why Admiral Tryon gave the order that he did, nor who or what people saw at the Tryon house that evening.

◆ *A Vision of Death* ◆

[C]an the death of another somehow be "foreseen"? Wing Commander George Potter of Britain's Royal Air Force certainly thought so.

During World War II, Wing Commander Potter was one of a group of British pilots stationed in Egypt. It was their job to bomb German ships bringing supplies to the German troops in North Africa. The missions were flown mostly at night and they were extremely dangerous.

One evening Wing Commander Potter and his friend Reg Lamb were in the officers' mess having a drink. Another group of officers was sitting in the room. Among them was a wing

commander called Roy. The group Roy was with suddenly burst out laughing, as if someone had told a joke. Potter turned toward the noise, and what he saw terrified him.

Roy's head and shoulders were moving slowly in a bottomless depth of blue-blackness. His lips were drawn back from his teeth in a dreadful grin; he had eye sockets but no eyes; the remaining flesh of his face was blotched with greenish purplish shadows.

Reg Lamb began tugging at his companion's sleeve. "What's the matter? You've turned white as a sheet ... as if you've seen a ghost."

"I have seen a ghost," said Potter. "It's Roy. Roy has the mark of death on him!"

Lamb saw nothing unusual, but Potter was still shaking. He knew that Roy was scheduled to be flying the next night. He thought of asking that Roy be taken off the mission, but such a request would certainly have been denied. In the end he decided there was nothing he could do.

The following night Potter got the message he had been fearing and expecting. Roy and his crew had been shot down and forced to ditch in the ocean. But there was some hope. Another plane had seen the men climbing into a life raft.

Potter told himself that the men would be rescued and his vision of death would be proved wrong. But as the hours dragged on there was no sign of Roy and his crew.

"And then I knew what I had seen," said Potter. "The blue-black nothingness was the Mediterranean at night and Roy was floating somewhere in it dead, with just his head and shoulders held up by his life jacket."

The Phantom
◆ Hitchhiker ◆

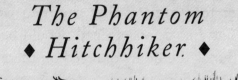

This may be the most widely told ghost story in the world. Here is the version that I first heard when I was growing up in Chicago.

A young man who had been out of town on a business trip was driving back to his home in Chicago. He was very tired, the hour was late, and a light rain was falling. The road was dark and deserted and he had to strain his eyes to see where he was going. Suddenly his headlights caught something white at the side of the road. As he drew closer he saw that it was a young girl, perhaps seventeen or eighteen years old, wearing a white dress.

The girl wasn't exactly hitchhiking, she was just standing there by the side of the road in the rain, and she certainly looked as if she needed a ride.

The young man stopped his car and asked the girl where she wanted to go. She gave him an address in town. It wasn't far, and he was going in that direction anyway, so he told her to get in.

The car he was driving was a two-door model, and the girl asked if she could climb into the back seat and take a short nap, as she was very tired. That was fine with the driver, and as she climbed in he saw how wet and cold she was. He took off his jacket and handed it to her. She accepted the offer gratefully.

The trip took about half an hour. The young man pulled up in front of the address he had been given. "Well, here we are," he said. There was no response. He turned around and looked in the back seat. It was empty.

That was impossible! He hadn't stopped once since the girl got in the car; there was no earthly way she could have gotten out. Yet she was gone.

He went up to the door of the house and knocked. Eventually, a rather sad-faced woman wearing a bathrobe came to the door. She looked vaguely familiar. The young man apologized for disturbing her at such a late hour, but said that something very strange had happened, and he had to tell her about it. He related the incident exactly as it had happened. The sad-faced woman did not look shocked or surprised. She just nodded sympathetically. And when he was finished she said, "You're not the first young man who's come to the door with this story. The girl you picked up is my daughter. She has been dead for ten years. She was killed in a car accident on that road where you found her. It happened on a rainy night just like this one—she was coming home late from a party, and she was wearing her white dress. I think she's still trying to come home."

The young man was stunned. He didn't know what to say. He mumbled his sympathy and rushed back to his car, telling himself that it was a bad dream. Then he realized his jacket was missing—he had given it to the girl in the white dress.

The following morning he went to the local

cemetery and found the dead girl's grave. There, draped across the headstone, was his jacket.

Similar tales about hitchhikers who vanish mysteriously have been told by hundreds, perhaps thousands of people. Is it all make-believe, or is there some other explanation?